BY YOURSELF

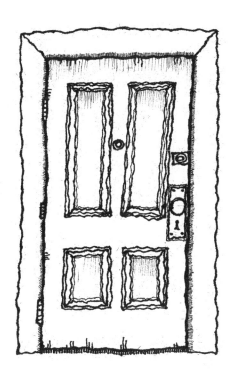

BY

YOURSELF

by Sara Gilbert
illustrated by Heidi Johanna Selig

Lothrop, Lee & Shepard Books   New York

Library of Congress Cataloging in Publication Data

Gilbert, Sara D.
    By yourself.

    Includes index.
    Summary: Presents tips for keeping house, caring for clothing,
preparing food, managing time, being safe, and entertaining oneself
for children who spend time alone at home. Includes pointers for
parents.
    1. Children of working parents—United States—Juvenile
literature.   2. Parent and child—Juvenile literature.   3. Self-reliance
in children—Juvenile literature.   4. Creative activities and seat
work—Juvenile literature.   5. Children—Time management—
Juvenile literature.   [1. Children of working parents.   2. Home
economics.   3. Cookery.   4. Self-reliance]   I. Selig, Heidi Johanna,
ill.   II. Title.
HQ792.U5G495   1983   640'.24054   82-13962
ISBN 0-688-01687-1 (lib. bdg.)
ISBN 0-688-01688-X (pbk.)

From one "by yourself kid" to another

CONTENTS

1. WHO ARE YOU?

If you are like millions of other American kids, you probably spend part of almost every day at home alone while the adults you live with are away.

Maybe work is the reason. Half of all the children in this country live with two parents who both hold jobs because they need the money or because it makes them happy, or for both reasons. Millions more live with one parent who must work outside the home to support the family. Because job hours hardly ever match school hours, and may even be at night and on weekends, many children take care of themselves during those times.

Sometimes hard-working parents like to relax and have fun away from home, and they leave their kids behind when they go out.

If you are old enough to read this book, you are probably old enough to take care of yourself at least some of the time. In the following pages you will find out how to do it a little better, and maybe how to like it a bit more—being **By Yourself.**

2. HOW DO YOU FEEL?

How do you feel about being by yourself?

Many kids feel angry. Even though they understand that their parents have good reasons for being away from home, being "deserted" makes them mad.

Many kids feel scared. They may not be scared of anything specific. Instead, simply the fact that there is no adult around makes them nervous.

Many kids feel sad. No matter why they're home by themselves, they suspect that their parents really want to get away from them. Or they worry that working parents must earn money **because** of them, and that makes them unhappy.

Many kids feel lonely. They can't seem to find anything to do and are sure that if only an adult were home, time wouldn't pass so slowly.

Many kids feel proud. They feel good that their parents trust them enough to leave them by themselves. They are also proud of all the things they've learned to do for themselves and for their families.

Having any of these feelings is okay. It's also okay—and not even surprising—to have more than one, or even all, of these feelings at once.

Where Do Your Feelings Go?

Sometimes people who feel bad about being by themselves let that feeling out the "back door" or the "side door." They may, for example, test their parents by going out without telling where they will be. This may be a way of saying, "Now that you are not at home, do you love me enough to worry about me?"

Or they may "accidentally" hurt themselves or get into scrapes. This can be an odd way of saying, "You see, I can't take care of myself, and if you stay away, I'm going to hurt you by hurting myself."

Challenges, like refusing to share in even the simplest tasks or to obey even the most basic rules, are another way unhappy or angry feelings can leak out. Unfortunately, whining, fussing, and fighting only make **everybody** angrier.

So if you are **mad** or **sad,** let those feelings out the "front door" by talking about them rather than by acting in ways that make time with parents unpleasant. Try saying what's really troubling you. Something like "I wish you didn't have to be away so much" will get your feelings out into the open so you'll feel better. With a parent, maybe you can work out some new plan for your time alone that will make both of you happier.

If you are **scared** or **lonely,** talk to a parent about how you feel and do your best to solve all the problems that worry you. Begin by thinking of interesting ways to spend your time (see page 14). Then go through your house or apartment as described in Chapter 6 to see if it passes the safety test. This may be all you need to feel more secure.

If you feel **proud,** you should! Doing a good job of being by yourself is a sign of growing up. But don't try to do everything for yourself; asking for help is never anything to be ashamed of. Just remember that even when parents aren't home, they are still ready and able to lend a hand.

Your Parents' Feelings

Parents have feelings and needs, too. When work or play takes them away from their children, they may respond in many different ways.

If work makes them tired, or bored, or angry, they may need to have people be a little extra nice to them when they come home. You can help by not leaving your things in a mess or, even better, by pitching in more!

If work makes them proud or excited, they may need someone to talk to. That someone can be you. After you have listened to your parents, you can tell them what happened in your own time alone that made you proud of excited. Or, if you have something on your mind that troubles you, now's the time to talk about it.

Of course, parents love their kids even when they're not with them. If they don't know where their children are or whether they're safe, they may become upset or angry. For your parents' peace of mind and for your own protection, you should always follow safety rules and stay in touch when you are by yourself. Chapters 6 and 7 will remind you how.

Naturally, parents hope their children will be happy taking care of themselves. They may worry that time alone will be time spent glued to the TV. If the hours creep by when you're by yourself, try some of the suggestions on the next pages. Remember the old saying? Well, it's true: time **does** pass quickly when you're having fun.

3. ENTERTAINING YOURSELF AND OTHERS

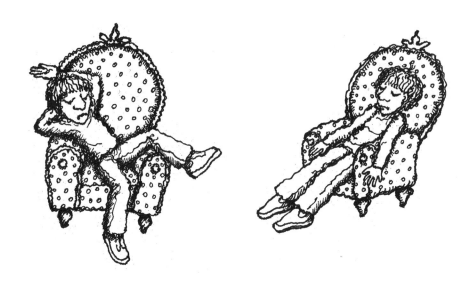

"But there's nothing to do!"

How many times have you made that complaint? Of course, there is **always** something to do—by yourself, with brothers and sisters, or with friends. (And with adults away, there's no one to say, "Quiet down!" or "I hope you're going to clean up that mess!") Chances are, even when parents are around you don't play **with** them; you probably just pump them for ideas. Well, use your own thinking cap. Here are some activities to get you started.

Independent Action

You can be sure to have fun by yourself if you . . .

. . . Plan some projects:

In a corner of your bedroom or in a spare room, keep one of your favorite pastimes in the works. When there's always a model to finish, a dress to sew, clay to sculpt, a picture to paint, woodworking to sand, a sweater to knit, a science experiment to explore, or a jigsaw puzzle to complete, your free time will be forever full.

Photography is a terrific by-yourself hobby. You can take pictures indoors and out, and when you become more expert, you can do your own developing. Gardening is great, too. If you have a backyard or field, dig up a corner and plant the flowers, fruits, and vegetables you like. If you live in an apartment, you can start a window box or be an indoor gardener with potted plants. Your library will have books that tell you all you need to know about these and other satisfying by-yourself projects. (**Tip:** Whatever you begin, the tidier you keep your work area, the happier everyone will be!)

. . . Make long-distance friends:

Amateur radio operators ("hams") talk to friends all over the world—with no phone bills! If you're interested, a local ham club can fill you in on all the details. A pen pal is another way to make friends. You can meet a lot of interesting people by mail, and a pen pal is someone to "talk to" whenever you're by yourself. You can usually find lists of names and addresses of kids who want to correspond in hobby magazines and in some magazines especially for young people.

What about those magazines? Browse through the selection at your local library or newsstand to see if there are any you might want to subscribe to. You might be especially interested in the ones listed on the next page. A subscription means you can often look forward to receiving mail, and you'll always have something new to read that you're sure to like.

Look for these general interest magazines in your library or at a large newsstand. Subscription cost and information will be included in each issue. Otherwise you can write to the subscription department at the address listed below. You may also want to check out the many special interest magazines devoted to almost every hobby, from sewing to science fiction, model building to sports-car racing.

Especially for kids

Boys' Life
Boy Scouts of America
1325 Walnut Hill Lane
Irving, Texas 75062

Cobblestone
Box 959
Farmingdale, New Hampshire 11737

Cricket Magazine
Box 2670
Boulder, Colorado 80322

Ebony, Jr!
Johnson Publishing Company, Inc.
820 South Michigan Avenue
Chicago, Illinois 60605

Highlights for Children
2500 West 5th Avenue
P.O. Box 269
Columbus, Ohio 43216

National Geographic World
National Geographic Society
17th and M Streets, N.W.
Washington, D.C. 20036

Ranger Rick's Nature Magazine
National Wildlife Federation
1412 16th Street N.W.
Washington, D.C. 20036

Stone Soup
The Magazine by Children
Box 83
Santa Cruz, California 95063

3-2-1 Contact
P.O. Box 2933
Boulder, Colorado 80321

For every age

National Geographic
National Geographic Society
17th and M Streets, N.W.
Washington, D.C. 20036

Newsweek
10100 Santa Monica Boulevard
Los Angeles, California 90067

Smithsonian
P.O. Box 2955
Boulder, Colorado 80322

Time
541 North Fairbanks Court
Chicago, Illinois 60611

. . . Start collecting:

Lots of kids enjoy collecting stamps, cards, coins, comics, dolls, rocks, butterflies, bottle caps—you name it; almost anything can be collected. Once you get started, you'll probably find that tracking down, organizing, and reading about your treasures can take more time than even **you** have to spare. What interests you? How about model trains or racing cars? Those are collectibles that you can play with as well! Remember, there are sure to be other kids with hoards like yours, so you're likely to find magazines, clubs, and pen pals to share your hobby with.

. . . Gather games:

Many activities are designed for one player: cards, puzzles, video and electronic games, for instance. If friends, brothers, or sisters are not around, try playing your favorite board games alone, too. By taking both sides in Monopoly, checkers, chess, backgammon, or whatever game is popular among your friends and family, you can get enough practice to be a real pro! (**Tip:** Set aside a handy shelf, box, or drawer for your games to keep all the pieces in one place.)

. . . Keep a book going:

What's your favorite kind of book? Mystery, fantasy, adventure, sports, science fiction, animal stories—any reading you enjoy can be entertaining and keep you company. So always keep your bookshelves stocked by visiting your library regularly (ask the librarian for ideas when you run out) and perhaps by joining a book club. If there's no book club in your school, write to any of those listed on page 19. They will keep you well read at low cost.

Looking for a good book? Here are some old and new favorites by authors popular with many kids. Your library or local bookstore is sure to know about these as well as other titles by the same author. Most are available in hardcover as well as paperback. Perhaps you will want to add some of them to your home library. A good book can never be reread too often!

The Book of Three by Lloyd Alexander
The Wizard of Oz by L. Frank Baum
Tales of a Fourth Grade Nothing by Judy Blume
A Bear Called Paddington by Michael Bond
Henry Huggins by Beverly Cleary
Me and the Terrible Two by Ellen Conford
Charlie and the Chocolate Factory by Roald Dahl
The Great Brain by John D. Fitzgerald
And Then What Happened, Paul Revere by Jean Fritz
Elidor by Alan Garner
Thirteen Ways to Sink a Sub by Jamie Gilson
Deadline for McGurk by E.W. Hildick
A Wrinkle in Time by Madeleine L'Engle
Chronicles of Narnia (series) by C.S. Lewis
Miss Pickerell Goes to Mars by Ellen MacGregor

The Borrowers by Mary Norton
Lizard Music by Daniel Pinkwater
The Westing Game by Ellen Raskin
Henry Reed, Inc. by Keith Robertson
Where the Sidewalk Ends by Shel Silverstein
All-of-a-Kind Family by Sydney Taylor
Charlotte's Web by E.B. White
Little House in the Big Woods by Laura Ingalls Wilder
Danny Dunn, Time Traveler by Jay Williams and Raymond Abrashkin

series by various authors
Alfred Hitchcock and the Three Investigators (published by Random House)
Landmark Books (published by Random House)
Choose-Your-Own Adventure books (published by Bantam)

Most of these are fantasy, adventure, and family-story books. If you're especially interested in one subject, like sports, or science, or animals, ask your librarian to point you toward the right shelves!

These book clubs will keep you and your mailbox busy:

Hardcover

Children's Choice Book Club
730 Broadway
New York, New York 10003

Weekly Reader Children's Book Club
245 Long Hill Road
Middletown, Connecticut 06457

Paperback

Scholastic Book Clubs
730 Broadway
New York, New York 10003

Troll Book Clubs
320 Rt. 17
Mahwah, New Jersey 07430

Xerox Paperback Book Clubs
245 Long Hill Road
Middletown, Connecticut 06457

Children's books are also offered through the Book-of-the-Month
Club, the Literary Guild, and the Better Homes & Gardens Book Club.
If the adults in your family are members of these clubs, you might
want to check out their selections.

. . . Exercise:

By setting up a "gym" indoors, you can burn up energy and get in shape without leaving the comforts of home. Turn your basement or other suitable room into a health club with a mat or old rug, jump rope, chinning bar, punching bag, light weights (or canned food for weights), and maybe even an exercise bike. Be sure you know how to use all the equipment safely. Try playing music from a radio or tape deck to keep your workout rhythm going. Indoor or outdoor basketball nets, a dart board, and a blank wall for handball are also good by-yourself energy eaters.

Finding Company

You need not be alone when you are "by yourself," of course. You can share good times . . .

. . . With brothers and sisters:

Some kids who have younger brothers or sisters think they're too little to bother with. But even the littlest ones can be good company when they're given a chance. You can teach them how to play many of your favorite games or let them help out with one of your hobbies. Sometimes, too, it's fun to play **their** games. You may think you've outgrown mud pies, paper dolls, sandbox projects, hide-and-seek, or similar activities until you discover how much you enjoy doing those things again. (P.S. Little brothers and sisters will think you're terrific for spending time with them.)

If you have older brothers and sisters, they may have that same "too little" opinion of you! If you show an interest in their activities or ask for their help with yours—and if you're not a pest—you'll find that they are happy to include you in their pastimes.

. . . With friends:

Nearly anything that you can do alone, you can do with friends. In fact, the more interests you get involved with, the more new friends you're sure to make. And the more you have going on in your home, the more these friends will want to join you there. So if visitors are allowed at your house when an adult isn't around, invite your pals over! (Some parents don't want their kids to visit a home where there isn't an adult, though, so it's a good idea to make it clear that you **are** by yourself.)

When others kids do come over, remember that house rules (see page 57) are for guests, too. It's smart to post them someplace where everyone will see them (and understand them). Company that can follow rules, play safely, and help you clean up afterward is company parents are happy for you to invite back. If, however, your parents would rather not have young guests when they are not around, arrange for some special days or evenings when friends can visit.

. . . With a pet:

A dog or cat can be a great companion, but some parents aren't too keen about them. If yours aren't, tropical fish or caged birds, hamsters, or gerbils are easy to care for once you know how (your local pet store is a good source for advice and guidance)—and they can be surprisingly good company. Of course, you will have to be responsible for whatever pet you get; but if you really enjoy animals, taking care of one shouldn't be too painful.

Lots of people like to feed birds, too. Buy or build a feeder for your backyard or windowsill and keep it stocked with feed. Soon, even if you live high up in an apartment building, you'll have a flock of "regulars" that are glad to see you. Learning about your feathered friends and their habits may soon become a new hobby.

. . . With interesting "noise":

A radio, records, or tapes can make your house seem less empty. Don't forget, though, that neighbors may not want to listen, too.

Money Matters

Fine, you say—but who pays for your good times? It's true that many of the games, hobbies, and activities suggested so far cost a little bit and a few are rather expensive, at least at the start; but most parents are happy to invest some money in materials to keep their kids interested and busy while they're away. Yours are likely to be more agreeable, though, if you offer to chip in.

You don't have to have a regular, "proper" job to earn some money. You can find work—for every day or just now and then—even in your own neighborhood. You could walk dogs, for example, water gardens, mow lawns, baby-sit, deliver newspapers, help out in a store, office, or playground, or do extra chores for pay in your own home. Put your mind to it, and you're sure to come up with lots of moneymaking ideas. Working is another way to make time alone fly by. Before you sign up for any kind of job, though, check with your parents—and be prepared to stick with it!

Other Business

"Do I have to do my homework?"

"Do I have to dump the trash?"

"Do I have to walk the dog?"

The answer to that kind of question is almost always "Yes!" We all have some things to do each day that we'd prefer not to do. When you are by yourself, it's up to **you** to get them done without being nagged or reminded.

It's often easier to fit everything in if you make a list or schedule of what you **have** to do and what you **want** to do. You might, for example, sit down with a parent and work out

```
3:30  Get home, call Mom
       Check message board
       Snack
       Walk dog
4:30  Do homework or chores
5:00  Free time
5:30  Set table
       Get out supper stuff
       Empty trash
6:30  Mom home
```

a general plan for your time alone. Questions you might talk about include:

> How much TV and what shows may you watch?
>
> How much time must you spend on homework before you break for something else?
>
> What chores must you get done before you go outside?
>
> How late may you stay out?

If you work out a good balance between your "want to's" and "have to's," you'll find that even the yuckiest tasks don't seem so awful.

Getting Out

As long as a parent knows—and approves of—where you are, you will probably be able to go out in the daytime when you're by yourself. Friends, with their family's okay, may ask you to visit. Or there may be afternoon groups, programs, or clubs at your school, activities at the local Y, 4-H, or community center, or informal teams at nearby fields or playgrounds that interest you. Just be sure your family knows where to find you when you go out, especially if they think you are at home. Even if you often spend time outside your house, you should always leave a note about where you've gone.

Remember to take your keys with you. How about attaching them to a chain on your belt loop or around your neck where they'll be hard to lose? You should always carry identification, too, which should include your name, address, and phone number **plus** the number or location where your parents can be reached. The name and phone number of your doctor might be a good item to list, too. You might keep your ID in a wallet, or on "dog tags" around your neck, or in any secure place where it can be found easily in case of accident or illness. Finally, even if you don't plan to go far, tuck in change for a telephone call and perhaps for a bus ride home. You never know when it might be a lifesaver.

Entertaining Checklist

You won't be bored by yourself if you:

- Keep some long-term projects going.
- Become a letter writer.
- Visit your library regularly or subscribe to a book club or magazine, or both.
- Have some games on hand that just one person can play.
- Build a collection.
- Have a special place at home where you can work out.
- Keep busy with brothers and sisters.
- Invite friends over—if it's okay with your parents and theirs.
- Get a pet.
- Keep yourself company with a radio, records, or tapes.
- Sign on for after-school work around your house or in your neighborhood.
- Go out to friends' homes or to wherever your favorite after-school groups meet; keep parents posted.
- Plan a schedule to organize your time.
- Use your imagination!

4. HELPING OUT

You may have noticed that the sample schedule on page 23 includes some housework.

Housework, you say. Good grief!

Well, think about it for a moment. First of all, there may be chores that you, like almost all kids, have to do. You are probably supposed to keep your room neat, for instance. Or you may be asked to help with a few tasks, like dishes, trash, yard work, or pet care. Why not do those things when you are by yourself?

Then, too, housework is a good way to help a working parent. Parents with jobs away from home may not have time or energy left over for jobs around the house. Why not lend a hand, or two? Let's take a look at those must-be-done chores and how your busy family might manage them.

Making Arrangements

Some working parents demand a lot of help from their children; others ask for very little. How do you know what's a fair share? If you have no time for the things you want to do, your duty list is probably too long. Another sign of an unfair share is having **many** more responsibilities than your friends, neighbors, or classmates, which makes you unhappy.

Before talking things over with a parent, make up a list of everything you do during the day and another list of what you don't have time for. You and your parent might then decide that some jobs aren't really very important. Maybe dishes can be done only once a day, for instance. Or maybe extra dust doesn't matter as long as your place looks neat. Or maybe things don't **have** to be neat!

You might discover from your lists that it's not the number of jobs but the jobs themselves that make you miserable. Baby-sitting for younger brothers and sisters might be too difficult, for example, or laundry might be too heavy or too hard to handle by yourself. In that case, agreeing to do different chores may solve your problem.

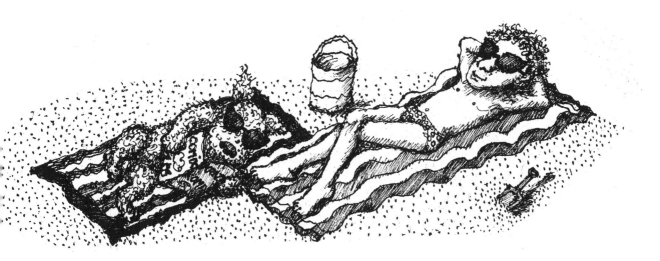

On the other hand, if it seems to you that are you are doing too **little,** and that an away-from-home parent could use some help, don't be afraid to say that, either! Draw up a schedule to figure out how much time you can spare for chores and offer to do those that suit you best.

You might also be happier (or less unhappy) about chores if you can get paid for some of them. Maybe your parent will accept a deal like this: as long as you keep up with your daily tasks, like keeping your room neat, you will get paid so much for special duties like mowing the lawn or doing the laundry. As with any other paying job, however, you will be expected to do them regularly and stick with them. (**Tip:** Don't forget to keep track of the hours you work and the jobs you do each day!)

How To Do It

Whatever arrangements you make within your family, you'll need to know how to do the jobs you take on. Here are some basic pointers for familiar tasks.

First and most important: for your own safety and to prevent breakdowns, make sure that you know how to work all equipment and which supplies to use. It's a good idea to attach a sheet of instructions to the dishwasher, washing machine, dryer, and other appliances you are likely to need. Do you know what to do if the vacuum cleaner clogs, for instance? Or how to change the bag when it's full? Do you know what cleaning agents are good for some jobs—and not for others? Unless you're sure, you could do more harm than good, and maybe hurt yourself as well.

Doing dishes

Whether you wash dishes by hand or in a machine, you should first scrape the stuck-on food into the garbage and rinse each piece with running water. A rubber mat on the bottom of the sink or a plastic tub in it will help prevent breakage. Use enough but not too much soap (in the dishwasher, be sure you use only dishwasher soap, in the right amount) and the hottest water you can stand (try wearing rubber gloves). Clean each piece with a cloth or a brush and rinse it under hot running water; then put it in a drainer. It's usually best to dry glass and metal things with a towel, but everything else can drip dry. Pots and pans are easier to clean after they've soaked for a while. They should be dried off, too, and put away.

Even if you're not in charge of the dishwashing process, you can be a big help if you rinse off every dish you use and put it in the sink, on the counter, or in the dishwasher.

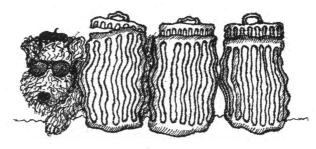

Dumping trash

It's a good idea to keep food garbage in a plastic bag separate from non-food trash. If you have a garbage disposal or a trash compactor, be sure you know how to use it safely and what items may not be put into it. Newspapers and magazines should also be gathered separately; they can make a trash bag awfully heavy. If there is a recycling center or program in your neighborhood, you'll need to sort paper, glass, and metal items. Why not keep three bags, labeled for each type, in a large container in the kitchen to make this job easier?

Different communities have different rules and schedules for trash collection. Find out what yours are so that you can load the cans shortly before they're to be emptied. If you have garbage to haul, watch out for leaky bags, or you'll have a yucky mess to clean up. And, of course, make sure that trash-can tops are on tight and that the area around the cans is neat to keep away unwelcome four-legged visitors.

Caring for clothes

One of the hardest things for many kids—and even adults!—to remember (or care about) is to hang their clothes up when they change after a busy day, but it can be a real help in keeping both the house and the clothes neat. It is especially important to hang up clothing that is damp from rain or sweat. Make sure there are plenty of hooks handy in the bathroom, kitchen, or laundry room so that you can hang things up to dry instead of flinging them into soggy piles. If food, paint, or other stains get on your clothes, soak them in **cold** water as soon as possible. This makes them much easier to clean later on.

If you are the person in charge of laundry, your first job on wash day will be to separate colored clothes from white ones and, if possible, light-colored things from darker ones (dark colors are more

likely to run and ruin the others). You might also want to divide delicate (thin blouses) and permanent-press (men's shirts) stuff from sturdier garments (towels). Using whatever products you've been told about—in the right amount!—wash dark clothes in cool or warm water and white ones in hot. If the machine you use has different cycles, delicate and permanent-press garments should go through the gentler cycles.

If you dry clothes on a line, make sure they're firmly attached. In a machine dryer, use hot temperatures for heavy clothing and cooler ones for lighter-weight things. Pay attention to the time the clothes stay in the dryer. If you take them out just when the dryer stops and shake and lay them (or hang them) neatly, less ironing will need to be done.

Before using a Laundromat alone, go several times with a parent to get the hang of it. You may have to sit there for the whole washing and drying process, so take along something to read or do. If it's okay for you to leave, keep your eye on the clock so that you can get back just when the machine stops. Otherwise, someone may mix up or even take your clothes.

Does anything need ironing? Most clothes don't these days. But if some of yours do, have an expert show you how to press shirts, pants, dresses, and flat items. Then when you feel ready to try it alone, make sure the iron is set to the proper temperature; too much heat can destroy some fabrics and too little heat may not do any good. **Never** leave an iron sitting flat on a piece of clothing. **Always** make sure it is turned off **and** unplugged when you are through.

Cleaning house

There are appliances and furniture to be dusted and polished, walls to be wiped, clutter to be cleared, and dirt to be swept or vacuumed. If you do any or all of these chores, remember to be certain about how the equipment works and which cleaning products to use. Then, the basic rule is "top to bottom": there's no point in sweeping or washing the floor before wiping walls, dusting, or dumping trash, because they all mess up the floor. Cleaning a wall, a mirror, or appliances from top to bottom means you can catch any drips as you work your way down. When you are by yourself, however, you shouldn't clean anything you have to climb to reach—and stay inside the windows! (**Tip:** Taking a few minutes to decide what should be done first will **save** you time in the long run.)

Even if you aren't the main cleaning person in your household, you can do your part. Pick up after yourself, for example. Be sure trash ends up in the basket. Make your bed presentable each morning simply by pulling the sheets and blankets up tight and smoothing the cover over it. Leave towels and washcloths hanging neatly after you've used the bathroom, and wipe out any mess in the tub or sink. Little things like these can make a place nicer for everyone to come home to and easier to clean, too.

Caring for pets

Whether your pet lives inside or out, always be sure it has enough water to drink and is fed on a regular schedule. Cages for rabbits, birds, hamsters, gerbils, and similar animals need cleaning every day; so do cat boxes. Fish tanks need cleaning, too; unfiltered water should be changed every couple of days, and filters

should be washed every few weeks. Most dogs need baths every few months (or whenever they get sticky or smelly). You can do this in a washtub, under the hose, or in the shower. Use a mild soap, keep the lather out of your pet's eyes, and be sure to rinse thoroughly. (**Tip:** The dog won't shake itself until its ears get wet.)

Your pet relies on you for its safety, too. Even if dogs are allowed to roam in your area, for instance, you will probably feel better if yours stays in the yard or on a leash. Whenever your pet is outdoors, make sure it is wearing a collar and ID tags, even in your own backyard.

If your dog or cat ever runs away from you, think of your own safety first. You could get hurt chasing after a pet into a busy street, and hunting for it without leaving word may worry your parent. Be wise and call the local pound or humane society as soon as you can with a description of the runaway; they're better trained in tracking down pets than you are.

If your pet ever gets hurt when you're by yourself, don't touch it or try to pick it up without wrapping it in some heavy cloth—a towel, blanket, or jacket will do fine. With one hand, close the animal's mouth, or hold the animal away from you while you carry it to a bathroom, kitchen, garage, or some other small enclosed space for safekeeping; even the most loving pet will attack when frightened or in pain. When you have, or come home to, a sick or injured pet, call a parent, a helpful neighbor, or a vet for advice. It may be hard to listen to your pet's cries of pain, but treating it yourself may do more harm than good.

Errands and shopping

These jobs take a surprising amount of time and energy, but they can also be fun—and you can learn some useful skills by doing them, too. If you live in the suburbs or the country where a car is needed to get to stores, you probably won't be able to run errands by yourself, but you **can** help out when a parent makes the trip.

Whether you are in charge or not, here are some tricks that you'll find save you in more ways than one:

• **Take a list.** If you have a lot of errands, you can count on forgetting one of them unless they're written down. In the grocery store it's all too easy to be tempted by what you don't need and let slip what you do need without a list to remind you.

• **Plan your tasks.** Dropping off dry cleaning before picking up repaired shoes, for instance, makes more sense than the other way around. Save the grocery store for your last stop; otherwise ice cream and frozen foods will melt and other food might spoil before you get home. Always think ahead.

• **Be careful with your money.** Carry it carefully—deep in a pocket where it can't fall out, or in a purse that's easy to hold on to. Count your change wherever you go. Some shopkeepers are careless, and some, sad to say, will think that because you are young, you can be fooled.

• **Learn to "comparison shop."** When you first start buying groceries, your parents will probably tell you exactly what brand, size, or variety to get. Soon, though, **you** will know how to pick out the best value by comparing price, size, and quality. You'll also learn that foods you make from scratch, whether snacks or main courses, are usually a lot less expensive than instants and packages. Naturally, not wasting money in the supermarket leaves more to be spent on more interesting things. So there's a real payoff to buying wisely.

Outside work

You may want, or be asked, to keep your yard neat, clip hedges, mow the lawn, rake leaves, shovel snow, or the like. Of course, you should get full instructions from a parent before beginning any of these. And you will be much better off if you avoid power tools or ladders when you're alone.

Keep a telephone near a door or window when you're outside so that you're more likely to hear it; or leave word with a parent about where you are (or both). If your family locks the house even when someone's in the yard, remember to do so. Put the key in your pocket, or wear it around your neck inside your shirt where it won't get in the way.

In hot weather, light clothing and a hat (even if you feel dumb in it) can help keep you cool. Drink lots of liquids, too, because hard work in the heat can make your body lose fluids fast. If it's very cold outside, wear clothing warm enough to make you sweat just a little while you work. Whatever the weather, old gloves, shoes or boots, and long pants and sleeves will protect you from scrapes, scratches, and blisters.

Baby-sitting

You may have younger brothers or sisters who need care when there is no parent around. If you feel confident about doing this and are used to it, fine. Just be sure you know all about schedules, food, and what to do in emergencies. When, for example, a baby or young child vomits, seems hot or flushed, or cries or sleeps more than usual, it may be a sign of illness. If you notice any of these symptoms, or if a child accidentally gets more than a small bump or scratch, you should call a parent, an adult neighbor, or your doctor for advice. When you're responsible for people besides yourself, it's especially important to keep these and other emergency numbers handy. See page 56.

How much should you do? You probably don't need to entertain little ones every minute, any more than a parent would. Some of the time, however, you may want to play games with them and their playmates, organize games or playacting, read aloud or tell stories, or

35

help with projects or homework. With a parent's help, gather toys and games that are right for kids their age, and make sure there's a supply of healthful snacks on hand for nibbles. Then you can simply supervise without having to be a part of their activities. A playpen, crib, or walker can keep a baby or toddler happy and safe; otherwise these tiny ones do have to be watched every minute. No matter how easy baby-sitting seems, remember that you cannot completely ignore the kids, even if they seem trustworthy. You must know where they are and what they're doing all the time. They should not go outside, for instance, or leave the yard without asking you. And you can't suddenly lose interest and stop the job, either; if you are put in charge, you must stay in charge. Your life might be a little easier if a parent makes it clear to the little ones that when you are baby-sitting, you are the boss. Even then, however, the job may still prove to be too much for you to handle. If so, ask a parent to try to work out some other child-care arrangement that will make the whole family happy.

Work Together

Wouldn't it be nice if none of these jobs had to be done at all? But they do. If everyone does his or her part, though—separately and together—the most tiresome of chores can be almost bearable. And it leaves more time for your family to spend on more exciting, enjoyable activities.

Helping-Out Checklist

However much housework you do:

- Decide with a parent what chores are right for you.
- Speak up if you think you're doing too much or too little.
- Learn how to use all cleaning appliances and supplies.
- Think safety first.
- Keep an instruction sheet near equipment you will be using.
- If you work outside, make sure the phone is where you'll be able to hear it.
- Even small tasks, like making beds, can make a difference—don't overlook them.
- Smile!

5. EATING WELL

Eating well is an important part of helping out and of taking care of yourself, because the right kind of food will make both you and your family feel good and stay healthy. But wait! Many people think that the "right kind" of food is boring food, or that they can eat well only when their parents feed them. That's not true; a lot of good foods are fun and easy to fix; for some, you don't even need a stove.

To Cook or Not To Cook?

A kitchen can be a dangerous place, and you may not be allowed to cook at all when you're by yourself. Your parents, like many others, may worry about fire and about burns from the stove or oven, as well as about cuts from sharp knives or other tools. If you really want to cook, however, don't give up! You'll find plenty of ideas in this book for no-cook meals and snacks. If you spend time in the kitchen helping out a cooking parent, you'll learn a lot of the tricks of the trade, and you may soon convince a worried adult that you **can** handle the kitchen on your own.

Even if you can cook by yourself, it's a good idea to try out your by-yourself foods when a parent is home. Whip up a batch of oatmeal cookies, perhaps, or cook and slice the sandwich meat—even bake the bread—so that you and your parent will feel confident about your kitchen smarts. Practice heating up cooked foods in the toaster oven or microwave, and make sure you know how to use the stove and other kitchen equipment, including knives and hot pads, safely. Many schools and organizations offer cooking classes for boys and girls; maybe one of them is right for you.

No-Cook Cooking

You don't have to use any kind of stove to be able to fix tasty foods for yourself, your friends, or your family. Here are some ideas.

Breakfast

Is the chef in your house gone before you leave for school or in too much of a hurry to feed you? Don't skip breakfast! If you do, you won't feel well or do well during the day. You could have milk and cold cereal, of course, or munch a sweet roll, but those foods are expensive, boring after a while, and not as good for you as some other fast breakfasts. Instead . . .

> . . . **Make a sandwich:**
>
> Hard-boiled eggs, cold meat, cheese, peanut butter, and cream cheese are easy and delicious fillings. Try whole wheat, rye, raisin, and date-nut breads for variety. With milk or fruit juice, a sandwich is a great way to start the day, and if you grab an orange or a banana, it's a breakfast you can carry with you on your way to school.

. . . Use up leftovers:

If you really liked last night's supper, have some of it cold for breakfast. Chicken, chops, even stew or macaroni and cheese may not be everybody's idea of what you're "supposed to" eat for breakfast, but why not? They make a better meal than a lot of the so-called breakfast foods.

. . . Make french toast:

With a parent in advance, soak bread slices in a mixture of eggs and milk, cook in a buttered skillet, wrap in plastic wrap, and freeze. You can reheat a slice at a time in the toaster and eat it with honey or syrup (or on the run with jelly).

. . . Shake an eggnog:

Stir an egg or two in a jar; add a little milk, honey, and perhaps some flavoring like vanilla; screw on the jar lid and shake well. Drink it straight from the jar, with or without a straw.

. . . Eat and run:

When you're **really** in a rush, grab some cheese, meat, a hard-boiled egg, or your favorite flavor of yogurt and a piece of fruit—and go. Don't bother with sugary foods or drinks (why even have them around?). Not only are they costly, but your body doesn't get much nourishment from them.

Lunch

Brown-bag or tin-box lunches are easy to make either early in the morning or the night before. They can be as predictable as peanut butter and jelly or as fancy as leftover lasagne. Let's begin with . . .

. . . Sandwiches:

By using different kinds of bread, fillings, and extras, you can add a bit of interest to your meal. Pita pockets, for example, make good, sturdy sandwiches and are available in the bread section of most grocery stores. You can get small ones and fill several with different fillings. Rye bread and the firmer loaves of "regular" bread are less likely to get soggy than those that are soft to begin with.

What you put between the bread depends, of course, on you. Why not be creative and practical at the same time? Yesterday's pot roast, baked fish, or broiled chicken when sliced makes a wonderful sandwich for today. Or help a parent roast a piece of meat or poultry in advance, slice it, wrap sandwich-size portions in individual plastic bags, and freeze. You can put the slices, still frozen, into your sandwich; by lunchtime they'll be fine. Also, they'll be a lot better for you than bologna or other processed meats that contain a lot of chemicals. And when you compare the cost, you'll find that home-cooked meats are a **lot** cheaper (just think what you and your family could spend that extra money on!). You'll find other sandwich-filling ideas on page 43.

You'll have a tidier lunch if you put the wet stuff on the inside: spread peanut butter on each slice of bread before you spread the jelly, for example, or put lettuce between the bread and gooey fillings like tuna, egg, or chicken salad. If you like tomato on your sandwiches, either wrap the slices in a separate plastic bag or place thin, nonjuicy slices between layers of meat or cheese so that the bread doesn't dissolve from the tomato liquid.

The way your sandwich is wrapped is important, too. It doesn't matter (in spite of what the ads say) what brand or form you use, but the more neatly and snugly sealed your sandwich is, the more appetizing your lunch will be. If you use waxed paper, tin foil, or plastic wrap, pretend you're wrapping a gift: fold the sides of the wrapping down tight, make triangles of the ends, and fold the ends neatly back toward the opposite side of the sandwich (as shown). If you use waxed paper or

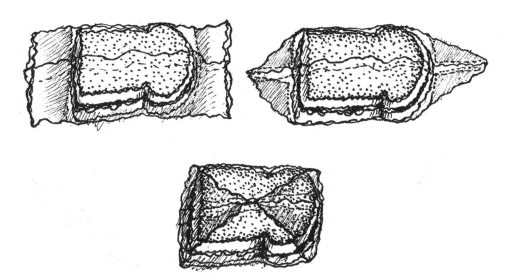

plastic bags, close them as tightly as you can. Use a piece of tape on waxed-paper bags and a twist tie on the plastic ones (even those designed to fold over). For really gooey sandwiches or for those made the night before, your best bet is to first wrap them firmly in tin foil and then to slip them into a sandwich bag.

Sandwich Fillings

Here's your chance to be a real inventor. Everybody knows about tuna or chopped chicken, egg, or turkey mixed with mayonnaise and a little chopped celery, but you've probably never tried those old standards with any or all of these:

      cut-up olives
      Thousand Island dressing
      diced apple
      capers
      tomatoes
      relish
      pickles
      nuts

Everybody knows about peanut butter and jelly, but for a change, try:

      peanut butter and banana
      peanut butter and bacon
      peanut butter and pickles
      peanut butter and any kind of jam or jelly **but** grape:
            strawberry, apricot, peach, marmalade
      jelly and cream cheese
      jelly and butter
      jelly and cottage cheese

Any sandwich will taste new if you use a different kind of dressing. Experiment with various types of mustard. Or try relish instead of butter. Or use one spread on one slice of bread (you **are** sampling different breads, aren't you?) and another on the other.

Greenery in a sandwich doesn't have to be lettuce. Sprouts, sliced cucumber or squash, or chopped green pepper are tasty variations on the green theme.

. . . Think about other main courses:

A hard-boiled egg, cold chicken, turkey, chops, or other meat, a cup of yogurt, cold pizza, a plastic container of salad or leftover casserole can all be easily packed the night before because there's no sandwich bread to get soggy.

If you get a wide-mouthed, insulated container, you can even carry a hot lunch: soup, stew, spaghetti, chop suey—almost any of your favorite foods. (Don't forget a plastic spoon or fork!) To keep your meal hot, run hot water in the container for a few minutes before filling it.

Dress up a hot or cold lunch with small packets of olives, pickles, carrot and celery sticks, rolls, or any other frills you like. Make sure you have all your lunch when noontime rolls around by tightly closing all the dishes you carry and setting them upright in the bottom of your lunchbox or bag.

. . . Don't forget dessert!

Fresh fruit (wrap the softer kinds separately), raisins, dates, dried apricots, oatmeal cookies, banana cake, or other goodies you make at home, or a covered dish of pudding, canned fruit, or last night's dessert can make your packed meal extra special.

(**Tip:** Plan ahead for packing. Keep little cans of juice in the fridge, or use an insulated container for juice or milk if you can't get them at school. Store the containers in the refrigerator, too, to keep liquids really cold. You might buy a small insulated bag, which keeps foods fresher than a lunchbox or paper bag, and it's easy to stuff in your schoolbag when it's empty. For no cost at all, you can collect small packets of salt, pepper, ketchup, and other condiments from carry-out restaurants to spice up your packed lunch. Carry-out restaurants and delis are also good sources for plastic utensils.)

Snacks

Packaged chips, candy, cookies, and soda are rough on the wallet and do little for you. Still, you'll want to have something around to give you a boost after school. Too much snacking, of course, can take away your appetite for more important eating at mealtimes, but with good-for-you snacks in the house, parents are less likely to say no to between-meal nibbling. So . . .

. . . **Keep a stock of sandwich fillings on hand** (see page 43).

. . . **Keep healthful snack foods around:**

Fresh and dried fruit; cut-up carrots, celery, and other vegetables in a plastic bag; nuts and popcorn or a homemade munch mix of dry cereals, nuts, and raisins (much yummier than chips!); yogurt; popsicles made from fruit juice; and graham crackers or homemade cookies are good for between meals. When supplies run low, add them to the grocery list you have posted in your kitchen.

Hot Snacks in a Snap

Spread tomato sauce on an English muffin. Top with sliced mozzarella and grated Parmesan. Broil in a toaster oven for instant pizza.

Bake any soft cookie, like oatmeal, or bar cookie, like gingerbread, for a few minutes in a toaster oven. Great for a cold winter day!

Spread mustard, mayonnaise, or ketchup on your favorite bread. Layer on sliced **cooked** meat or hard-boiled eggs, and maybe a slice of tomato or onion. Top with sliced cheese and broil until the cheese melts.

If your tap water is hot enough, you may be able to make instant soups and hot cereals without having to worry about boiling the water. Add your own flavorings, such as grated cheese or croutons for soup or raisins for cereal.

. . . Try different kinds of canned food:

Lots of kids like tuna, chicken, or deviled ham eaten with tiny breads or crackers. Experiment! Canned fruit packed in juice instead of sugar syrup is good, too, by itself or with yogurt or cereal.

. . . Drinks are snacks, too:

Instead of soda, try lemonade and other fruit drinks. Chocolate syrup in milk, or cocoa mix that makes cocoa in hot tap water taste good, too.

Feeding the Family

If you want to help an away-from-home cook with a big meal, you have lots of chances, even if you aren't allowed to use the stove. For example . . .

. . . You can be in charge of salads.

In a large bowl, wash and cut up greens like lettuce, celery, cucumbers, and green peppers; then cover and put the mixture in the refrigerator without any dressing. Presto—you've made a big part of the meal. For variety you might add olives, bean sprouts, diced fruit, tomatoes, or cooked or raw vegetables such as squash, beans, broccoli, cauliflower—almost anything that tastes good and looks pretty. A salad can be a whole meal, too, when you add cheese, meat, fish, cooked egg, or leftovers like pasta or crumbled bacon. What a treat for the end of the day!

. . . Lots of desserts need no cooking.

Instant pudding, whole or cut-up fruits, yogurt, and ice-cream parfaits or sundaes are simple and nearly everybody's favorite treats. If you want to be really fancy, make a pie using a no-cook pudding or ice-cream filling and a ready-made graham-cracker crust.

. . . When a parent is home, both of you can fix meals for a whole week.

Together, you can cook your family's favorite foods and freeze them. Then, when you're by yourself, you can take the evening meal out of the freezer to have it ready for reheating.

. . . Or you (and your brothers and sisters) can get everything ready for cooking and serving.

You can, for example, pull the meat or main dish from the freezer, wash the vegetables, or make a casserole except for the cooking. You can set the table, too—paper plates, cups, mats, and napkins may make cleanup easier (but every now and then surprise the family with a really fancy table!). A list on the refrigerator can help you keep track of whose turn it is to do what, and what to do when, so that fresh foods don't sit out for too long and frozen ones have enough time to thaw. And, of course, you or any other family member who doesn't feel handy in the cooking department can help by clearing the table and cleaning up.

Behind the Stove

Once you are allowed to cook, you'll discover it has many advantages. Not only is it fun, but it's also a sure way to get what **you** like to eat. (**Tip:** If you do the cooking, you can probably make a deal with someone else to do the dishes—and you know that cooking has got to be more fun than that!)

You might feel more comfortable in the kitchen if supplies and equipment are geared to your size. For instance, put basic tools—

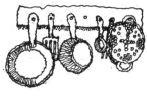

measuring cups, cooking spoons and forks, bowls, cutting boards, and the like—in drawers and shelves low enough for you to reach easily. Have a low work table in the kitchen if there's room, or a steady, sturdy step stool that brings you safely up to counter height. Though most foods are more economical to buy in large containers, they can be hard to handle and easy to drop; so how about storing milk and juice in smaller bottles, and flour, sugar, and other foods in tins or jars that you can manage? Also, small pans are easier to lift and will fit in a toaster oven if you're nervous about using the stove. So keep a supply of tin-foil baking pans on hand, and use lightweight skillets and saucepans whenever possible (no-stick surfaces will make cooking and cleaning even easier).

Of course, just because you have a parent's okay to use the stove doesn't mean you have to spend every afternoon sweating over it for hours. You can still fix the tasty no-cook meals described earlier in this chapter. But every once in a while impress your family with a special cooked-by-you main course or even with a whole meal. Start with something simple: scrambled eggs, salads, hamburgers, spaghetti, or macaroni and cheese (if you don't have a simple recipe, follow the

Eggs Make Any Meal

With a fork, beat two eggs per person in a bowl. For **breakfast,** cook the eggs over low heat in a greased or no-stick pan, stirring with a wooden spoon until they're done. For **lunch or supper,** before adding the eggs heat any or all of the following until partly cooked: diced or chopped onions, green peppers, mushrooms, sausages, or other cooked meats. When the eggs are half done (wet-looking), add a tablespoon or so of grated cheese (such as Swiss, Parmesan, or mozzarella—or even cream or cottage cheese) and maybe a pinch of your favorite herbs and spices (such as parsley, dill, or garlic). For extra zip or a dash of color, top the finished eggs with a bit of tomato sauce, a sprinkling of croutons, or a shake or two of paprika or chili powder.

directions on the pasta box). Hot sandwiches are a good change of pace, with a salad; or try soup, cheese, warm bread, and salad. You can broil chicken or fish with almost no trouble, using different seasonings, like chili powder or mustard, to jazz them up. Or get really creative with a casserole: invent your own combination of meats, vegetables, rice, or pasta and mix in a can of soup or other sauce; top with cheese or bread crumbs and bake!

All-in-One Super Casserole

1. Mix one or more of these: 1–2 cups canned or cooked fish, chicken, turkey, ham, or other meat, with one of these condensed soups: cream of mushroom, cream of celery, cream of chicken, tomato.
2. Add 1 soup can water or milk and 1–2 cups one or more of these: leftover, canned, or unthawed frozen vegetables (carrots, green beans, celery, broccoli, or zucchini are good choices), partly cooked or leftover macaroni, noodles, or rice.
3. Top with one or more of these: crumbled crackers, corn chips, or potato chips; wheat germ; dry cereal; grated Parmesan or other cheese.
4. Bake in a covered casserole dish at 325° for ½ hour or until bubbly.

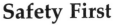

Safety First

- Always cut away from you and strike matches away from you.
- Put food on a cutting board and slice down.
- Never reach **over** a lighted burner.
- Keep pot handles turned inward.
- Use hot pads to protect your hands and kitchen surfaces.
- Two hands are safer than one.

When you feel ready to try fancy menus, explore the cookbooks in your home or in the public library. Some excellent ones that contain recipes with very detailed instructions for beginning cooks are listed on the next page. Here are some tips to make your cookbook cooking a success:

- Read the recipe **all the way through** first.
- Then check these points: How many servings does the recipe make? Is it enough or too much for your family? How long will it take to make **and** to cook? Do you have all the ingredients you need?
- Spread waxed paper or newspaper on the counter or floor for easy cleanup later.
- Get all the ingredients out, ready, and measured.
- If you use up any foods, add them to the grocery list you have posted.
- Turn on the oven to the temperature called for in the recipe.
- Get ready any pans you will need.
- Follow the recipe **in the order described** in the recipe (this is especially important when you're baking so that the chemistry works right, but it's a good idea for other types of cooking as well).
- Set a timer for the cooking time given in the recipe (if you haven't got a timer, use an alarm clock). All cooks think they can remember when to take a dish out of the oven or off the stove; most cooks forget at least once and end up with a burned mess.

Unfortunately, most cookbooks especially for kids are either cutesy (Mickey Mouse Salad) or limited to only one kind of cookery (vegetarian, for example). There are a few exceptions, of course. You are much better off, though, with one of the many hefty cookbooks published for adults. Don't be put off by the small print or thickness of the book—many contain simple, tasty recipes and good step-by-step directions. Some old standbys are *Joy of Cooking, Betty Crocker's Cookbook,* and *Ladies Home Journal Cookbook.* More recent volumes, such as *The Family Circle Cookbook,* also include valuable nutrition information.

If you haven't any of these at home, look for them in a bookstore, your library, or at a friend's house. When you are buying a cookbook, remember that although a hardcover is more expensive than a paperback, it probably has better pictures—which are useful to new cooks and experienced ones as well—and it will last through many more mealtimes than a paperback. Not sure about spending a lot on a cookbook? Then borrow it from the library or a friend and try it out. (This is an especially good idea if you are curious about anything but a general cookbook—one that has recipes for only one kind of food, for instance, like Mexican dishes or desserts; or one that is devoted only to fancy dishes.) The most important feature to look for in any cookbook is clear, step-by-step instructions for each recipe from beginning to end: oven temperature, needed pans, and number of servings first; ingredients and measurements next; then processes for cooking.

As you become a more expert cook, try comparing recipes for the same dish and then coming up with your own version. Cooking is far more interesting and fun if you don't just cook, but create as well.

Don't Stop Now!

Don't forget: the last step in cooking, whether you use the stove or not, is straightening up. This means putting away the food you've used, throwing the scraps into the garbage, rinsing or soaking the dirty dishes, pots, and pans, and cleaning the counter tops. Then you're ready to begin all over again.

Eating-Well Checklist

You can eat well by yourself if you:

- Know how to use tools and equipment safely.
- Spend time in the kitchen with the cook in your family.
- Sign up for an in-school or after-school cooking class.
- Try any of the simple meals and recipes included in this chapter.
- Help with shopping or cooking so that your house is always stocked with foods that are easy, fun, and good to eat.
- Learn to use cookbook recipes. Start with simple foods and then experiment with your own concoctions.
- Offer to help with meals in other ways than cooking.
- Add foods that you use up to the grocery list.
- Always clean up after yourself!

53

6. FEELING SAFE

When you are by yourself, you need to stay safe. But it is just as important to **feel** safe. Many kids worry about ghosts, or burglars, or creepy things that might be hiding in dark places or that might sneak into the house. If you have worries like these, you probably know they don't make sense—but that doesn't make them go away.

There are some things that you can do, however, that might.

Check Out the House

You won't get the by-yourself jitters if you are familiar with all the nooks and crannies—and ins and outs—of your house or apartment when you are **not** alone.

Are there any dark corners or strange noises that bother you? Ask about them. You won't think your house is haunted if you know that the clanking sound is just the radiator heating up, for instance. And once you find out that the mysterious door in the basement just leads to a closet, it shouldn't trouble you anymore. If you feel silly talking about such things, remember that **everybody** gets nervous sometimes.

Could anybody sneak into your house or apartment? Even if you know they couldn't, you will feel more secure if you and a parent have tested the locks on all the doors and windows to make sure that they can't be opened from the outside, especially those at ground level or next to a porch roof or fire escape. If you have a chain lock, peephole, or window by the door, you know you won't let the wrong person in by mistake. That is important, too!

Now, can **you** work all the locks you have to? Try it! Can you lock the doors and windows? Can you unlock them easily? If you can't, have a parent make them less stiff or sticky.

Do your keys open the door from the outside without a fight? Practice! Sometimes keys are tricky. Have a parent show you the "secrets" of your home's locks and keys.

What should you do if the lights go out? What should you do if you are too hot or too cold when you are by yourself? Learn how to operate the heat and light systems in your home. If you know how to change a fuse or throw a circuit breaker, you'll never have to worry about being alone in the dark. If you know how to turn the heat or cooling system up or down, you can be sure you'll never have to sweat or shiver while waiting for a parent to come home.

Emergency Numbers
Police ....
Fire. ....
Ambulance ....
Poison Control .....
Dr. Wiswall ....
Management Office ...
Plumber. ....
Mom's work ....
Fynchon's no ....
Ellens no ....
Dans ho ....

Keep Help Handy

You will feel safer (and be safer, too!) if you know you can always get help in a hurry. You might need it for a big emergency or for some minor crisis (to turn the lights back on if you can't, for example, or to unlock the door if it is stuck). Sometimes you might just need someone to talk to if you are feeling lonely.

So attach these numbers to your phone or right next to it:

Emergency service numbers (see page 64), including police, fire, ambulance, and poison control

Numbers where adult family members can be reached

Your doctor's phone number

Repair-service numbers (or if you live in an apartment, the number of your building's superintendent)

Numbers of relatives who live close by

Numbers of neighbors who will help you when you are by yourself

If you do not have a telephone, it is important to know someone nearby who does. Even with a phone, though, you will probably feel safer knowing that there are people in your building, on the block, or just down the road to whom you can turn.

You and your family should get to know your neighbors to find out which ones are likely to be home when you are by yourself and which ones seem the most friendly and reliable. A parent can ask some of these people if they would be willing to act as backstops when you're alone. In exchange, you and your family might offer to baby-sit for them, run errands, help with housework or yard work, share food, tools, or other items, or watch their house when they are away. You might be surprised what you can do for your neighbors that would make their lives easier, too.

The Role of Rules

Mostly, though, you will be taking care of yourself. Rules can help. Many kids don't like the idea of rules. They think they're made up just to keep them from doing what they want to do, or that rules are only another way for parents to push them around.

But when you are by yourself, rules can help you to feel secure. In a way, rules can take the place of a parent who isn't around to remind you of what to do—and what not to do—in order to stay safe.

Every family has its own set of rules. One home may have dangers that another does not. Behavior that worries some parents may not bother others. Different children need different kinds of protection.

Someone in your family might want to write out the rules of your house and post them someplace handy for you and your guests. Or you might just talk them over to be sure everyone clearly understands them. However you do it, your "by-yourself" rules will probably answer these questions:

- What friends, if any, may you have over? What rules must they follow?
- Whom, if anyone, may you let into the house?
- Where, if anywhere, may you go by yourself?
- Must you lock the door when you go out, or may you leave it open?
- How closely should you stay in touch with a parent?
- What activities may you do and not do? For instance:
      How much TV?
      May you use the stove? The oven?
      May you use the fireplace? Fill the bathtub?
      May you use electric tools? Any tools?
- When must you start (or finish) your homework?
- How much time may you spend on the telephone?
- What foods are musts, maybes, and nevers?
- What chores, if any, must you get done and when?

If you think that some of your house rules are unfair or silly, or if you think, after being by yourself for a while, that some can or should be changed, talk with a parent about it. On the other hand, if you have rules that work, you won't be spending so much by-yourself time worrying about what you should or shouldn't be doing.

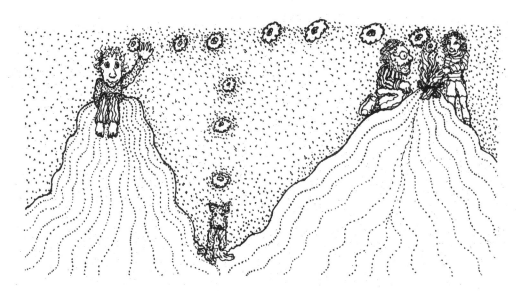

Stay in Touch

Not all families have the same plan for keeping tabs on one another. Any way you have, though, of checking in with a parent will make you feel safer and less alone.

When you are by yourself, do you know where your parents are and when you can expect them back? Whether parents are away at work or out for relaxation, you should always know how to reach them. Put this information by the phone; that way you can call them if you are sick or have a big emergency, or if you're just feeling lonely. (Parents feel more secure, too, knowing that their kids can and will phone if they have troubles.) Make sure your parents know how to reach **you** as well in case something happens to **them.**

It will also ease your worries (and a working parent's, too) if you telephone your mother or father as soon as you get home every day. Parents who don't have their own phone where they work often set a time when **they** will call home.

If your time-alone plans change—if you decide to visit a friend, for example, or if you are delayed getting home—it is very important to let an away-from-home parent know where you are. Kids sometimes feel that this kind of reporting is babyish. But think how frightened **you** would be if your parents didn't check in when **their** plans changed.

A "message center" in your home will help your family stay in close touch even when its members are separated. Yours might be a bulletin board near the phone, or a pad held by magnets to the refrigerator door or attached to the kitchen or hall table. Here's where you can find notes and reminders like "Don't forget to walk the dog," "Fix the salad late—I won't be home till 7:30," or "If you finish your homework, we can go to the game!" And here's where **you** can leave memos about any phone calls for a parent or where you've gone if you leave the house.

Using Your Head

You may feel safer if you figure out solutions to situations that seem scary or worrisome **before** they happen. Talk over some of these with a parent and see if you don't feel better afterward.

It's nighttime and you've been watching something on TV that turned out to be frightening. All of a sudden, every dark corner looks spooky and every noise gives you the creeps. What do you do?

- You could turn off the TV, turn on all the lights, and call a friend. A good idea.
- You could call a parent. But what if he or she isn't there? Instead of leaving word that you're in trouble (that could cause panic), ask that your parent call back, but say that it is **not** an emergency. Then call a friend or neighbor if you need someone to talk to right away.
- You could refuse to let yourself be scared and feel silly about phoning anyone—but it will seem forever until your parent comes home. Remember, it's okay to be scared, of imaginary things as well as real ones, and you should never feel funny about asking for help or support.

Your friend nags you to go to the movies one afternoon, but you can't reach a parent for permission. What do you?

- Do you say no and stay at home? That's one solution.
- Do you leave a note in the message center and then try again to get in touch with a parent on the way? That's another solution.
- Do you just go, knowing you'll be back before a parent gets home? Can you see why this is no solution? If you had an accident or other mishap, your parent wouldn't be able to know about it. Also, remember that someone's "disappearing" scares parents just as much as it does kids.

Your little sister is late getting home from school. What do you do?

- You could forget about it and assume she's stopped off at a friend's. But what if she hasn't?
- You call the school to find out if there's any reason for her to be late. A wise first step. Then call all her friends' homes to see if she's there; if not, ask their parents for help, and call a parent or neighbor, or both, so that these adults can take action as soon as possible.

Can ghosts or bogeymen come through walls? Of course they can't! But there are times when, alone, everybody wonders. So it's good to know how to trap those imaginary beings, as well as how to take charge when real trouble strikes, to keep away a bad case of jitters when you're by yourself.

Feeling-Safe Checklist

You will feel safe when you are by yourself if you:

- Explore your home when you are not by yourself.
- Learn how to work the locks on all the doors and windows.
- Know how to operate the lights and the heating and cooling systems.
- Can get help in a hurry—by phone or from neighbors—if you need it.
- Have house rules that everyone understands.
- Know how to reach a parent at all times.
- Think about and solve "what if" situations that give you the spooks.

7 STAYING SAFE

Even when parents are around, of course, fires can break out, accidents can happen, and people can cause problems. When your parents are not at home, though, it's up to you to know how to handle these dangers and emergencies.

The best way to do this is to think about how to cope with them in advance. Even if this seems scary, you are much less likely to run risks if you:

- Plan how to **escape** threats and to be rescued from them.
- Think about how to **prevent** problems.

Planning Escapes

When you are checking out the house with your parent for creaks and groans, make sure you know about all the safe exits (there should be at least two). Just as you will feel safer knowing that only you can get into your home, you will **be** safer if you know how to get yourself out quickly in case of disaster.

If you live in an apartment building, locate the fire escape for your apartment and make certain you can get to it easily. Taller, modern apartment houses are built to resist the spread of fire. In addition to their elevators, they should have at least one enclosed fire stair, and preferably two separate ones. Make sure you know where they are, too.

If you live in a private home, or in an apartment that is part of a private home, you should learn how to escape from each story of the building. If there is no safe way to climb down from an upper story, your family can buy an inexpensive, portable fire ladder that hangs over a windowsill and can be thrown down in an emergency.

Wherever you live, be sure you can work the locks quickly! Although for safety you may want to keep any easy way to enter your home well locked, remember that accidents can happen inside, too. Then you must be able to open those locks—on doors, windows, or metal gates—fast. Agree ahead of time where you will meet a parent after an escape—at a neighbor's house, at a neighborhood store, somewhere definite.

Keep a supply of battery-operated lights (**not** candles) and one or more inexpensive battery radios stored in a convenient, permanent place in several parts of your home. With a parent, check the batteries every so often, and never use them for everyday without replacing them. With battery-operated lights, you'll always be able to see even if an emergency happens at night or knocks out your electricity. A battery-operated radio will come in handy if you need news or weather bulletins during a power failure or other big event.

Practice! It isn't enough to know in your head where emergency exits are. You need to feel as comfortable with them and as familiar with them as you are with brushing your teeth. So when a parent is on hand, try some dry runs. If there are bugs in your system, you can figure out another in advance that will get you away from inside dangers speedily.

Preparing for Rescue

If trouble strikes when no adult is home, there are emergency numbers you should call first—even before contacting your family. For example, telephone companies in most cities or towns have special short numbers that you can dial to reach the fire department, police, or ambulance in a hurry. Learn these numbers. Keep them in a handy place near your phone, too. And remember, whether the crisis is a fire, a crime, or an accident, emergency people need to know **your address** and **your problem.** No matter how upset you are, you must be able to give that information clearly enough to be understood. "Please come!" or "Help!" or saying only your name isn't enough. Again, practicing with a parent helps. It might make you feel better to keep your address and simple directions for reaching your home posted next to the phone.

If your area of the country does not have special emergency numbers, or if for some reason you cannot use them, call the telephone operator when you need help quickly. To do this, dial or push the button for Operator—0—that is, the number 0, after the 9, not the letter O with MNO.

 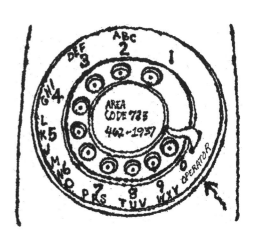

When the operator answers, first say, "This is an emergency." Although operators have been trained to handle emergency calls, they do not expect them as often as emergency services do. Once you've alerted the operator, tell your address, your phone number, and the problem.

Why not practice that now?

Can you find eight fire hazards here?

1. papers stacked near flammable liquid
2. candles lighted near curtains
3. door (escape route) blocked by a portable heater
4. iron left on
5. clothes basket near open-screened heater
6. window (escape route) blocked by table
7. frayed cord on iron
8. stove on when no one is in room

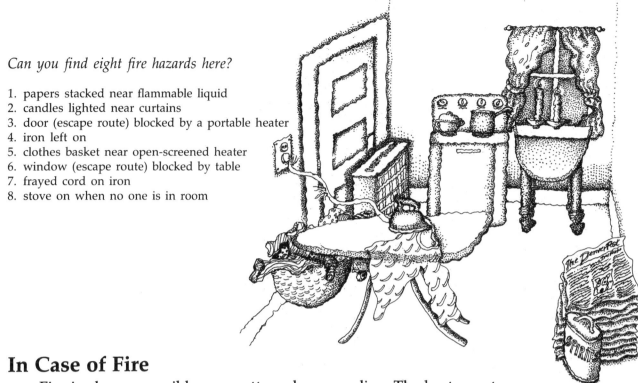

In Case of Fire

Fire is always possible, no matter where you live. The best way to avoid its dangers is to prevent it.

Matches or lighters are not toys. Except for lighting or relighting gas appliances, you should never use them when you are by yourself (and even then, only if a parent has said okay).

If you are allowed to cook, stay in the kitchen whenever something is on the stove, and use fairly low heat whenever possible. Even if you have an electric stove, the contents of a pan can catch fire if the heat gets too high or is left on too long.

Be sure you know how to operate your oven (if you may use it). A gas oven is especially tricky, because gas can build up inside it if the flame doesn't go on or if the "pilot light" goes out. Gas that leaks out unburned from a stove or any other appliance, such as a heater or clothes dryer, can be dangerous. But a chemical is added to the gas used for stoves that gives it a strong odor. When a parent is home, learn how this odor smells. If you smell it when you're by yourself, first make sure that all the knobs on the stove, heater, or other appliance are turned all the way off. If they are, check the pilot lights and relight them if they've gone out, **if** a parent has taught you how. Otherwise, ask for a neighbor's help. If the gas smell is unpleasantly strong, open the windows, too. If it is **very** strong, get yourself and anyone else out of the house fast and go for help.

Fires can also start in piles of trash, in places where paint or cleaning fluid is stored, and in worn or overloaded electrical wires and connections. When you're exploring your home with a parent, keep an eye out for these things and have them cleaned up or fixed before you're on your own. Smoldering ashes in fireplaces or trash burners can spark fires, too, so be sure these are safely enclosed. Of course, lighting a fire in them is a parent's job and not something you should be doing when you are by yourself. Save those marshmallows for another time!

But in case fire does break out, what is the **first** thing you and your brothers and sisters should do?

Get out.

Don't stop to call the fire department, don't try to gather up valuables (or even, sad to say, pets). Just leave by your escape route or any safe exit. Hiding from fire—in a closet, a bathroom, or anywhere—is impossible. The only safe place is **out.**

As you leave, feel each door before you open it; if it's hot, use another exit. Never use an elevator—always the stairs. Stay as close to the floor as you can (crawl or belly along if you have to) because smoke, which can be dangerous, tends to rise. To protect your face and hair, cover them with a wet towel, if possible. Otherwise pull your clothing over them. If your hair or clothing should ever catch fire, douse the flames by rolling on the ground or by wrapping a blanket around them. Once you're away from danger, you should call the fire department and your parents. Be sure, though, that you are completely safe before you do so.

The **only** kind of fire you should ever think about trying to put out by yourself is a small stove fire. If you cook, keep a pan lid and a box of baking soda handy. Then if the contents of a pan start flaming, put the lid on fast or dump soda on it. Don't use water; on an electric stove, that can be a disaster, and water does nothing for some kinds of fire.

1—2—3

No matter what happens to you when you are by yourself, you will have nothing to worry about if you remember these basics:

1. **Your safety comes first.** Nothing is more important than protecting yourself. Think ahead to prevent danger and to get yourself quickly away from a bad scene.
2. **Keep in touch.** Always be sure that a parent or some other adult knows where you are or how to find you.
3. **You are never alone.** There is certain to be someone around who can help you: the police or fire department, your neighbors, your friends, a parent. All you have to do is ask, and asking is nothing to be timid about.

Are You Hurt?

You can prevent accidents by using your head and by following house rules. Rules about what you may and may not do when you're by yourself are almost always for your own safety. Be smart and heed them.

Still, house rules can't cover everything, and that's where your commonsense come in. It tells you to be extra careful when you're around knives and sharp objects, appliances, and other tools, especially electrical equipment. The same goes for a heated oven or stove and bodies of water (including filled bathtubs). Water and electrical equipment are a dangerous combination, so you'll want to keep them apart. This means watching out for puddles and making sure you are not wet before plugging or unplugging something. Practicing mountain climbing when you're home alone is also a bad idea.

These warnings may be so obvious that they sound silly, but it's a good idea to be aware of them anyway, especially if you're in the house with younger brothers and sisters who may not be as sensible as you. Still, don't get too cocky; if you're about to try something new or something you don't feel sure about, stop and **think.** Maybe you're better off waiting until an adult comes home. For example:

Your ball gets stuck on the porch roof. What do you do?

- You find something else to do until an adult can lend a hand. Good!

- You get a good, sturdy ladder, have a friend stand by, and climb carefully up. Maybe, depending upon the friend and your porch.

- You climb out a window and totter across the roof. Never.

You're locked out because you forgot or lost your key, or let the door slam while the key is inside. What do you do?

- Do you climb in a window? Sure—if it's at ground level and if you don't have to break the glass. Otherwise, no. Of course, if your house is **too** easy to get into without a key, your family might have to rethink its security system.

- Do you go to a neighbor's and wait? Yes, but remember to call a parent and leave a message about where you are.

- Do you get an extra key from a neighbor or from the superintendent of your building? That's the best solution. Again, it requires thinking ahead.

But even the most careful and sensible people can have accidents. Before they happen to you, make sure that you have all first-aid supplies, like adhesive bandages and disinfectants, in one easy-to-reach place. Then practice these first-aid measures so that you know how to treat yourself (or friends or brothers or sisters) when you are by yourself.

Small wounds

"Small" means cuts and scrapes that hardly bleed at all. Wash them with soap and water, dry carefully, and cover with disinfectant and a bandage. If there is some bleeding, press a clean cloth or bandage on it hard. The bleeding should stop in a minute or so; then bandage the cut. (If the bleeding does not stop that quickly, get help.) Ice cubes also keep small bangs from turning into big bruises.

Little burns

Touching a hot pan, stove, or iron can create an instant red hurt. Rub a burn like this with an ice cube (or hold it under very cold water) and leave it bare. Soak a burn that is more than a sting—one that you got from a flame or big spark—in icy water while you call for help.

Bad cuts

For a cut that you know is deep, or that is bleeding a lot, grab the cleanest cloth you can find and press down very hard on the wound. At the same time, call your emergency numbers. If you are hurt and have to run for help, first tie a cloth very tightly around the bleeding spot.

Bad falls and other body blows

If someone takes a tumble and hits some part of their body—especially the head—very hard, have the person sit or lie still for a moment while you get help. If it happens to you when you are alone, lie down and then get up slowly. Wrap yourself in a blanket or something else warm, and get in touch with your emergency helpers.

Shocks

If you get a shock from any source of electricity, sit still and keep warm. If after a few minutes you feel dizzy or at all odd, or if you feel burned where the electricity made contact, call for help.

Poison

Swallowing anything that you think might be poisonous or harmful deserves a call to the poison-control number on your emergency list. The people there will want to know exactly what and how much was swallowed, so try to have this information ready. Then follow whatever instructions they give you. Last, call a parent.

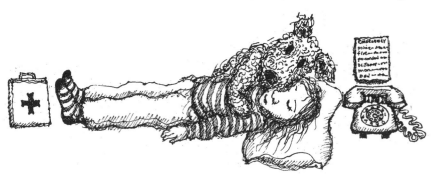

Medicine may not be exactly a poison (though it can be), but too much or the wrong kind can make you sick. So if someone feels sick—a headache, stomachache, or whatever—call a parent. Do not take any medicine until you have checked with an adult. Even if you get an okay, be certain that you know which one and what dose to take.

Knowing all of these emergency first-aid steps will help you cope should something go wrong when an adult isn't around. You might even want to take a first-aid course from your local Red Cross or Y, especially if you are going to be in charge of younger children. If you have a Red Cross or Scout manual, consider keeping it in your supply kit in case your memory blanks in an emergency.

Handling People Trouble

Some kinds of danger, sad to say, are posed by other people. These aren't nice to think about, but, as for other emergencies, the first way to deal with them is to prevent them. Think about these situations:

You answer the phone, and it's a wrong number. The caller says, "What number is this?" What do you do? Instead of giving out your number, say, "What number were you calling?" If an answer is given and it's not your number, simply say, "You have the wrong number." If the caller gives your number, you can reply, "Please check the number; there is no one here by that name." If the person wants to speak to a parent, make up an excuse about why he or she can't talk (in the shower, sleeping). Keep secret that you're home alone.

You answer the phone and you hear strange noises or a caller saying weird things or using bad words. What do you do? Hang up the phone, right away! If it happens only once, you can wait until someone comes home to talk about it, but if it happens more than once you should tell an adult about it right away.

Someone comes to your front door. What do you do? First, find out who it is before opening the door. This is easy if you have a chain lock, a peephole, or an intercom system. Maybe you'd like to suggest that these things be put in if you don't have them.

If the person at the door is making a delivery, you can take the package through the door. If it's someone who says he or she is there to make a repair, and your parent has not told you to expect anyone, close the door and phone your parent to check. A meter reader from the gas or electric company will have some kind of formal identification; don't feel shy about asking to see it before you let anyone in. If a parent-okayed repair person or other visitor makes you at all nervous, you'll feel better if you stay by the open door until he or she leaves. Naturally, no other strangers should be allowed into your home. Any visitor who seems to want to hang around, or who suggests that you go someplace else with him or her, is bad news. Get away from that person as fast as possible, even through your emergency exits, and call for help, if necessary.

Boo!

Some emergencies simply can't be prevented. The weather, for example, is always full of surprises. The best, and only, thing you can do is be prepared to cope with such unexpected events.

If the lights go out because of a power failure, carefully find your way to the emergency lights and battery radio. Lighting your way with candles or matches is a no-no. Use your flashlight to locate the phone and call a parent. First report what happened and get instructions. Then stay off the phone except for urgent calls so that you can be reached. If the phone doesn't work either, try to get to a neighbor. Otherwise, stay put. An all-news or emergency radio station will keep you posted if the blackout is widespread.

If a big storm—hurricane, tornado, or dangerous electrical storm—**is approaching,** check in with a parent. You may be better off at a neighbor's house (but if you go, make sure your parent knows), but if the storm has already hit, stay indoors (in a basement if possible) with your battery lights and radio handy.

If rescue crews take charge during a neighborhood or community crisis, follow their instructions. If this means you have to leave your house for some other shelter, do it. If you can't reach a parent first, leave notes and messages about where you are. Be sure you and your brothers and sisters have identification with you. This will make it much easier to get back together with your family later.

Luckily, disasters like these rarely, if ever, occur. Fortunately, most accidents and emergencies can be prevented. Nobody likes to think about all the possible dangers that can do harm, but planning and practicing what steps to take in case they occur is the best way to stay safe.

Staying-Safe Checklist

You will stay safe when you are by yourself if you:

- Know the escape routes from your home and how to use them.
- Make sure locks work easily so that you can exit quickly in an emergency.
- Decide, ahead of time, where you'll meet your family if you have to leave home to get away from danger.
- Store battery-operated lights and a battery radio in an easy-to-reach spot.
- Keep special emergency numbers near the phone.
- Know how to prevent and escape from fire.
- Follow house rules and use your head to keep accidents from happening.
- Have first-aid supplies on hand and know how to use them.
- Report strange phone calls or callers to a parent.
- Ask who's at the door before opening it and ask to see identification. Never let in anyone you don't know.
- Never tell a stranger that you're home alone.
- Think ahead!

8. POINTS FOR PARENTS

Parents who must leave their children at home alone understandably have a lot of worries. You will feel better about the situation if, first of all, you do everything you can to make sure your kids are safe.

• You can be sure they'll know how to get out of the house or apartment fast in an emergency if you go over escape routes and plan with them carefully. Practice these plans with fire and safety drills. Smoke alarms and good locks can be installed at very low cost.

• Your children will probably feel more secure if you establish firm rules for safety, geared to each child's age, personality, and skills. These should cover every possible hazard—fire, accident, strangers at the door, and any special dangers posed by your home or neighborhood. Even children who complain about rules really appreciate the concern they demonstrate.

• If you place emergency telephone numbers as well as numbers of dependable neighbors next to the phone, you can make certain your kids will be able to get help in a crisis.

• You will want to talk about safety in a way that will not frighten your children too much (you know best your own kids' fears and needs), but a little healthy respect for danger is not a bad thing.

• Any neighbor or nearby relative who acts as an emergency backstop for you should know the name and number of your pediatrician, should know where to reach you, **and** should have a medical authorization note signed by you that gives permission for emergency hospital care. Many doctors will not offer treatment beyond basic first aid without such permission.

• Don't feel that you are being overly fearful or nervous taking precautions like these. You are simply being sensible. And think how you would feel if an emergency **did** arise and you hadn't prepared for it!

When you are confident that your children can handle any problem, you will feel less anxious about leaving them home alone. There are some children, however, who will have difficulty on their own and who should **not** be left alone regularly if at all possible. A child, for example, who cannot read will have a hard time taking care of himself or herself. And a child with a mental or physical handicap or one whose health is poor should probably not stay home alone.

Giving young children full responsibility for even younger siblings is also not a good idea. It can be too much of a strain for the older child; it can present threats to the younger; and if anything happened to the younger ones, the emotional aftershock to the child in charge could be devastating.

What about a child who doesn't want to be left alone, but who doesn't want to tell you about his or her fears either? Watch for telltale symptoms, such as sleep disruptions (nightmares, insomnia, and the like), changes in eating patterns, school problems (getting in trouble at school, doing poorer work than usual, reluctance to go to school), "mysterious" physical ailments (aches in the stomach, head, or joints that have no physical cause; rashes; nervous tics), regressions (bed-wetting, other babyish behavior), and increased numbers of "accidents" when you are at home or away. If you notice any of these, try to find out what worry is behind them. Some simple shift in arrangements may make your child feel safer when home alone.

It may be that for such children, or for a child who for any other reason shouldn't be left alone, you will need to plan for care or companionship. Here are some alternatives you might want to consider:

• Hiring a sitter is a possibility, of course, though even if you can afford it, reliable people are sometimes very hard to find.

• Find out what day-care facilities are available in your community. If there aren't any, or if they are costly or crowded, urge your community organizations (or your employer) to begin one.

• Investigate any after-school programs run by your school system, community center, church or synagogue, or recreation department. If you don't find any, you can press to have one started.

• Get together with your friends, relatives, or neighbors. You will probably be able to find people you know who can and will watch your children, at your home or at theirs. You might pay a small fee, or you can perform services for them in return. For example, if neighbors keep your children during the afternoons, you can take charge of theirs some weekends and evenings. Or you can run errands for them or do other chores on a regular basis.

• See what you can do to have your work hours shifted. Offer to come to work early and give up your breaks so that you can leave sooner. More and more businesses, too, are allowing shared-time jobs and making other adaptations to the needs of working parents. Find out what your employer is willing to accept.

• If you incur any expenses in having your child cared for while you work, examine the current tax laws to see if that cost can be deducted from your tax payments. For more information contact the Day Care and Child Development Council of America, 711 14th Street N.W., Washington, D.C. 20005.

Kids feel better about being by themselves when they know that their parents do care. You have many ways of showing this, even when you are not at home. Set fair but firm rules for your children's behavior, for example, and enforce them. Keep in touch with your kids and be sure they can and will keep in touch with you. Make demands on your children, for sharing housework or doing their fair share of other tasks, but beware of overburdening them.

Remember that many children, depending on their age and circumstances, will "test" away-from-home parents, especially in the beginning. They may blatantly misbehave. They may stubbornly refuse to do chores they've always done. They may disappear for a while without leaving word or asking permission. This can be distressing and maddening, but it's important to remember that, in addition to correction, such behavior calls for honest talk. Your kids may well be angry at you for "leaving home." They may honestly fear that you no longer love them. So they need reassurance along with chastising.

Many working parents subtly reinforce their children's worries. They may, in fact, secretly believe that they are cheating their children. Even when they must work outside the home to support themselves and their family, they may feel guilty. Many experts feel, however, that not only do children of working parents frequently **not** suffer, but they gain in emotional strength, confidence, and independent skills. You can help ensure these benefits in several ways.

Begin by making sure that your children understand, by your words and your actions, that you are concerned about them and love them even when you are away from them. Do what you can always to be easy to reach when you are not at home. If you work, try to have your children visit you on the job and meet your co-workers.

Avoid going overboard with your children—overindulging, overrestricting, or overburdening them—because of your own fears and needs. Instead, enforce your guidelines for behavior firmly, and praise good behavior and independence.

Finally, spend "quality time" with your children. Set aside a period of each day when, no matter how tired or overworked you feel, you will concentrate on your children. Talk, play, listen; ask questions; share news. This needn't be a big event; just being together or sharing chores can make everyone feel closer. Maybe you can spend a good chunk of time with your children on days off or during vacation, sometimes doing what they want to do, sometimes doing what you want to do, and sometimes just doing nothing.

Many parents find that their relationship with their children improves as a result of being separated from them part-time. All it takes is care, they say. Maybe this will be true for you.

INDEX